METHOD IN THE STUDY
OF TOTEMISM

LECTOR HOUSE PUBLIC DOMAIN WORKS

METHOD IN THE STUDY OF TOTEMISM

ANDREW LANG

ISBN: 978-93-5614-369-2

Published: 1911

LECTOR HOUSE LLP
E-MAIL: lectorpublishing@gmail.com

METHOD IN THE STUDY OF TOTEMISM

BY

ANDREW LANG

1911

CONTENTS

METHOD IN THE STUDY
OF TOTEMISM

I.

Is there any human institution which can be safely called "Totemism"? Is there any possibility of defining, or even describing Totemism? Is it legitimate—is it even possible, with due regard for "methodology" and logic—to seek for the "normal" form of Totemism, and to trace it through many Protean changes, produced by various causes, social and speculative? I think it possible to discern the main type of Totemism, and to account for divergences.

Quite the opposite opinion appears to be held by Mr. H. H. Goldenweizer in his "Totemism, an Analytic Study."[1] This treatise is acutely critical and very welcome, as it enables British inquirers about totemism to see themselves as they appear "in larger other eyes than ours." Our common error, we learn, is this: "A feature salient in the totemic life of some community is seized upon only to be projected into the life of the remote past, and to be made the starting-point of the totemic process. The intermediary stages and secondary features are supplied from local evidence, by analogy with other communities, or 'in accordance with recognised principles of evolution' [what are they?] and of logic. The origin and development, thus arrived at, are then used as principles of interpretation of the present conditions. Not one step in the above method of attacking the problem of totemism is logically justifiable."[2]

As I am the unjustifiable sinner quoted in this extract,[3] I may observe that my words are cited from a harmless statement to the effect that a self-consistent "hypothesis," or "set of guesses," which colligates all the known facts in a problem, is better than a self-contradictory hypothesis which does not colligate the facts.

Now the "feature salient in the totemic life of some communities," which I "project into the life of the remote past," and "make the starting-point of the totemic process" is the totemic name, animal, vegetable, or what not, of the totem-kin.

In an attempt to construct a theory of the origin of totemism, the choice of the totemic name as a starting-point is logically justifiable, because the possession of a totemic name is, *universally,* the mark of a totem-kin; or, as most writers prefer to

---

[1] *Journal of American Folk-Lore*, April-June, 1910.
[2] *J. A. F.* p. 280.
[3] *Secret of the Totem*, p. 28.

say, "clan." How can you know that a clan is totemic, if it is not called by a totemic name? The second salient feature in the totemic life of some communities which I select as even prior to the totemic name, is the exogamy of the "clans" now bearing totemic names.

To these remarks Mr. Goldenweizer would reply (I put his ideas briefly) there are (1) exogamous clans without totemic names; and there are (2) clans with totemic names, but without exogamy.

To this I answer (1) that if his exogamous clan has not a totemic name, I do not quite see why it should be discussed in connection with totemism; but that many exogamous sets, bearing *not* totemic names, but local names or nicknames, can be proved to have at one time borne totemic names. Such exogamous sets, therefore, no longer bearing totemic names, are often demonstrably variations from the totemic type; and are not proofs that there is no such thing as a totemic type.

Secondly, I answer, in the almost unique case of "clans" bearing totemic names without being exogamous, that these "clans" have previously been exogamous, and have, under ascertained conditions, shuffled off exogamy. They are deviations from the prevalent type of clans with totemic names *plus* exogamy. They are exceptions to the rule, and, as such, they prove the rule. They are divergences from the type, and, as such, they prove the existence of the type from which they have diverged.

So far I can defend my own method: it starts from features that are universal, or demonstrably have been universal in totemism. There *is* "an organic unity of the features of totemism," — of these two features, the essential features.

Lastly, Mr. Goldenweizer accuses us "Britishers," as he calls us, of neglecting in our speculations the effects of "borrowing and diffusion, of assimilation and secondary associations of cultural elements, in primitive societies."[4]

This charge I do not understand. There has been much discussion of possibilities of the borrowing and diffusion and assimilation of phratries, exogamy, and of totemic institutions; and of "ethnic influences," influences of races, in Australia. But the absence of historical information, the almost purely mythical character of tribal legends (in North-West America going back to the Flood, in Australia, to the "Dream Time"), with our ignorance of Australian philology, prevent us in this field from reaching conclusions.

(Possibly philologists may yet cast some light on "ethnic influences" in Australia. The learned editor of *Anthropos*, Père Schmidt, tells me that he has made a study of Australian languages and believes that he has arrived at interesting results.)

Mr. Goldenweizer represents, though unofficially, the studies of many earnest inquirers of North America, whether British subjects, like Mr. Hill Tout, or American citizens such as Dr. Boas. They vary, to be sure, among themselves, as to theories, but they vary also from British speculators. They have personally and laboriously explored and loyally reported on totemism among the tribes of the

---

[4] *J. A. F.* p. 281.

north-west Pacific coast and *Hinterland*; totemism among these tribes has especially occupied them; whereas British anthropologists have chiefly, though by no means solely, devoted themselves to the many varieties of totemism exhibited by the natives of Australia. These Australian tribes are certainly on perhaps the lowest known human level of physical culture, whereas the tribes of British Columbia possess wealth, "towns," a currency (in blankets), rank (noble, free, unfree), realistic art, and heraldry as a mark of rank, and of degrees of wealth.

Mr. Goldenweizer's method is to contrast the North-Western American form of totemism with that prevalent in Central Australia, and to ask,—how, among so many differences, can you discover a type, an original norm? I answer that both in North-Western America and in Central Australia, we find differences which can be proved to arise from changes in physical and "cultural" conditions and from speculative ideas. I have said that in British Columbia the tribes are in a much more advanced state of culture than any Australian peoples, and their culture has affected their society and their totemism. Wealth, distinctions of rank, realistic art, with its result in heraldry as a mark of rank, and fixed residence in groups of houses are conditions unknown to the Australian tribes, and have necessarily provided divergences in totemic institutions. Mr. Goldenweizer replies "that the American conditions are due to the fact that the tribes of British Columbia are 'advanced' cannot be admitted."[5] But, admitted or not, it can be proved, as I hope to demonstrate.

---

[5] *J. A. F.* p. 287.

II.

Mr. Goldenweizer gives what he supposes some of us to regard as "essential characteristics" or "symptoms" of totemism. He numbers five of these "symptoms."

1. An exogamous clan.

2. A clan name derived from the totem.

3. A religious attitude towards the totem, as a "friend," "brother," "protector," &c.

4. Taboos or restrictions against the killing, eating (sometimes touching, seeing) of the totem.

5. A belief in descent from the totem.

Mr. Goldenweizer next, by drawing a contrast between British Columbian and Central Australian totemism, tries to prove, if I understand him, that "the various features of totemism," are, or may be "essentially independent of one another," "historically, or psychologically, or both."[6]

Now, looking at the five symptoms of totemism, I may repeat (speaking only for myself) that, as to 1 and 2, I think *the exogamous clan,* with "*a clan name derived from the totem*" is an institution of such very wide diffusion that I may blamelessly study it and attempt to account to myself for its existence. But this does not mean that I regard all exogamous social sets as at present totemic; or as always having borne totem names. Again, sets of people (I cannot call them "clans," for the word "clan" indicates persons claiming common descent from a male ancestor,—say *Clan Gihean, Clan Diarmaid*), may bear animal or vegetable or other such names, yet not be at present, as such, exogamous. Of these are the Arunta, and the Narran-ga.

3. *A religious attitude towards the totem.* One cannot discuss this without a definition of religion. "Totemism is not a religion," says Mr. Frazer, with whom I am here in agreement.

4. *Totemic taboos.* These, though extremely general, are not quite universal even in Australia.

5. *A belief in descent from the totem.*

This belief is post-totemic, being merely one of many aetiological myths by which men explain to themselves why they are totemists; what is the nature of the *rapport* between them and their totems; why they bear as a kin (or association) animal or vegetable names. One or another such myth is not an essential part of

[6] *J. A. F.* p. 183.

totemism, for it is, necessarily, post-totemic.

I am thus left confronting the problems, (1) why are the immense majority of exogamous kins, in societies which we call "totemic," named by animal and other such names; and (2) why are they exogamous?

As for other exogamous social sets, which bear, not animal names, but territorial, or descriptive names, or nicknames, often derisive, it is my business to show, if I can, that these sets, or some of them, have passed, in historical times, out of the stage of totem-kins, owing to circumstances which I shall describe. Next (2) I have to show, if I can, why a few sets of people, bearing, as sets or associations, animal or other such names, are now no longer *exogamous*.

If I succeed, I think that I may regard "Totemism" as characterised by exogamous kins bearing totemic names, and as "an integral phenomenon" existing in many various forms.[7]

If I understand Mr. Goldenweizer this attitude and effort of mine must seem to him "methodologically" erroneous, and "logically unjustifiable." "This attitude," he says (namely the attitude of those who hold totemism to be "an integral phenomenon"), "is reflected in the way several authors deal with the so-called 'survivals' of totemism, where from the presence in some region of one or two of the 'symptoms' of totemism, or of the fragments of such symptoms, they infer the existence in the past of totemism in its 'typical form,' that is, with all its essential characteristics."[8]

Thus, for example, from such phenomena as standards bearing animal forms; or from animal worship,—each animal being adored in its own district,—or from myths of descent from gods in the form of animals; or from the animal names of some Roman *gentes*; or from animals closely associated with gods (like the Shrew Mouse with Sminthian Apollo); or from the presence of beings partly theriomorphic partly anthropomorphic, in art, many writers infer a past of totemism in Italy; Israel; Greece Hellenic and Greece Minoan; in Egypt; in Ireland; and so forth. It is not my purpose to treat of such so-called survivals. I am to deal with peoples such as the tribes of Australia, New Guinea, and North-West America, who, if not the rose, have been near the rose: if not always totemic are at least neighbours of totemists.

---

[7] But I exclude from my treatment of the subject, the "Matrimonial Classes," or "sub-classes" of many Australian tribes, for these are peculiar to Australia, appear to be results of deliberate conscious enactment, and, though they bear animal names (when their names can be translated), have no traceable connection with totemism.

[8] *J. A. F.* p. 182.

III.

Mr. Goldenweizer tabulates the results of his comparison between the Totemism of British Columbia and that of Central Australia.[9] In the latter region the totemic institutions and myths are not those of South-Eastern Australia. To the totemism of many tribes in South-Eastern Australia that of a great tribe of British Columbia, the Tlingit, bears,—if we may trust some of the evidence,—the closest possible resemblance; while, if we trust other and conflicting evidence, the resemblance is, on an important point, nearer to the institutions of certain Australian tribes of the furthest south, in Cape Yorke peninsula. The evidence for British Columbian totemism, I shall show, is so wavering as to make criticism difficult. The

[9] *J. A. F.* p. 229. I give the tabular form in this note:

TOTEMISM IN BRITISH COLUMBIA AND CENTRAL AUSTRALIA		
	BRITISH COLUMBIA	CENTRAL AUSTRALIA
Exogamy (1)	Totemic phratries (Tlingit) Totemic clans (Haida, Tsimshian, Northern Kwakiutl)	Phratries Classes Totem Clans (generally not independent exogamous units.)
Totemic names (2)	Phratries (Tlingit) Clans (Haida) 1 of 4 clans (Tsimshian) Clans (Northern Kwakiutl)	All totem clans
Taboo (3)	Non-totemic taboo, common; totemic absent	Numerous totemic and non-totemic taboos
Descent from the totem (4)	Absent (Tlingit, Haida, Tsimshian) Occurs (Kwakiutl and farther South)	Universal
Magical ceremonies (5)	Not associated with totemism	Intimately associated with totemism.
Reincarnation (6)	Not associated with totemism	Intimately associated with totemism.
Guardian spirits (7)	Intimately associated with totemism	Not associated with totemism
Art (8)	Actively associated with totemism	Passively associated with totemism
Rank (9)	Conspicious (in individuals and groups)	Absent
Number of totems (10)	Small	Large

terminology, too, of some American students has been extremely perplexing. I am sorry to be obliged to dwell on this point, but a terminology which seems to apply five or six separate terms to the same social unit needs reform.

Dr. Boas is one of the most energetic field-anthropologists of the United States. To him we owe sixteen separate disquisitions and reports on the natives of the North-West Pacific coast and *Hinterland*, all of them cited by Mr. Goldenweizer in his excellent Bibliography. But Mr. Frazer observes that Dr. Boas variously denominates the kindred groups of the Kwakiutl tribe as "groups," "clans," "gentes," and "families." I must add that he also uses *gentes* as a synonym for phratries—"Phratries, viz. *gentes*."[10] Now a "phratry" is not a *gens*; a "group" may be anything you please; a "family" is not a *gens*;—a "*gens*" is an aggregate of families,—and a "clan" is not a "family."

Mr. Goldenweizer's tabulated form of his comparisons between British Columbia and Australia contains ten categories (see the last footnote of p. 6). Of these, two at least (8) (9) indicate elements which are purely proofs that the B.C. tribes are on a much higher, or later, level of social progress than the Australians. These two are *Rank* and *Art*. Had Mr. Goldenweizer added *Wealth* and *Towns* to his ten categories he would have given four factors in B.C. culture which affect B.C. totemism, and which do not exist in Central Australia, where realistic art is all but wholly unknown: art being occupied with archaic conventional patterns. Thus, in Australia, the bewildering B.C. heraldry—the "crests"—cannot, as in B.C., confuse the statements of observers, perplex their terminology (for they often use "crests" as synonyms of "totems"), and disorganise totemism itself. But we can find, not far from Australia, a parallel to this heraldry in New Guinea. For "crests" or badges in Central British New Guinea, see *Totemism and Exogamy*, vol. ii. pp. 42-44. The people, like the B.C. tribes, are settled in villages. They have "a number of exogamous clans," most clans occupying several villages, and they have paternal descent. "Every clan" (as apparently in some cases in British Columbia) "has a number of badges called Oaoa, which, generally speaking, may only be worn or used by members of the clan." The "clan" names are geographical or are patronymics, they are not totemic; the badges either represent birds and mammals, or are "schematised" from some prominent feature of these. The people are not now totemists, even if they have passed through totemism.

Again (category 5), in British Columbia, "Magical Ceremonies are not associated with Totemism." In Central Australia they are "intimately associated with totemism." Yes, but in South-Eastern Australia they are not, as far as our evidence informs us. Magical ceremonies are not in Mr. Goldenweizer's list of five symptoms or characteristic peculiarities of totemism, so I leave them out of account.

Again, as to Taboo (category 3), in British Columbia, "non-totemic taboo is common; totemic, absent."

As to this "absence," Mr. Frazer has a great deal to say. For example, we have Commander Mayne's book, *Four Years in British Columbia*, a work of 1862, in which is given information from Mr. William Duncan, a missionary among the Tsim-

[10] Franz Boas, *Fifth Report of the Committee on the North-Western Tribes of Canada*, p. 32, cited in *Totemism and Exogamy*, vol. iii. p. 319, note 2; cf. p. 321.

shian tribe. All such evidence given prior to controversies about totemism is valuable. According to this account, the Indians used, as "crests," representations of Whale, Porpoise, Eagle, Raven, Wolf, Frog, etc. Every person was obliged to marry out of the name of the animal represented by his crest, and each "clan" tabooed its animal, "will never kill the animal which he has adopted for his crest, or which belongs to him as his birthright," that is, apparently, his "familiar," and his inherited totem. This is original totemism in North-West America.

Mr. Frazer says, "So far as I remember, no other writer on these North-Western Indians has mentioned their reluctance to kill their totemic animals. In the course of this work I have repeatedly called attention to the paucity of information on this important side of totemism in the writings of American ethnologists."[11] Mr. Frazer also finds the usual totemic taboo among the Yuchi, a tribe of the Gulf nations.[12]

In Central Australia are "numerous totemic and non-totemic taboos." But in other parts of Australia there are also tribes where people even kill and eat their totems. The totemic taboo is an extremely common institution, but not a note *stantis vel cadentis ecclesiae.*

Another category is (4), "Descent from the Totem." As I have said, the belief in this descent is a mere explanatory myth to account for totemism; and, like all other such myths, could only arise after men were not only totemic, but wondered why they were totemic. Consequently such myths are not of the essence of totemism, and their varieties are of no importance.

The belief, or myth, of totemic descent is absent in British Columbia, says Mr. Goldenweizer, in the Tlingit, Haida, and Tsimshian tribes, and present "among the Kwakiutl and further south." In Central Australia descent from the totem is "universal."

But it is a queer kind of "descent," is not, in the usual sense, descent at all, and, notoriously, *is not descent by physical generation.*

Then we have the category (7), "Guardian Spirits, intimately associated with Totemism" in British Columbia, "*not* associated with it in Central Australia." Yet, in Central Australia, a man's spirit is a totemic spirit. Again (10), "Number of Totems." In British Columbia "small," in Central Australia "large." But it is "small" in such central regions of Australia as those of the Dieri and Urabunna, and in South-Eastern Australia; and why it is so large among the Arunta no man knows. It is an unexplained peculiarity, and not essential.

"Reincarnation" (6) is, in British Columbia, "not associated with Totemism," in Central Australia "intimately associated with Totemism." Here, Mr. Strehlow, for the Southern Arunta, reports otherwise; while for the Northern Arunta and other tribes, this "reincarnation" is part of a speculative explanatory myth. The myth, as I can show, explains, at one stroke, how men come to have souls, and why men are totemic We know the kind of savage philosophy which accounts for

---

[11] *Totemism and Exogamy,* vol. iii. pp. 309-311.

[12] F. G. Speck, *Ethnology of the Yuchi Indians,* Philadelphia, 1909, pp. 70 sq. *Totemism and Exogamy,* vol. iv. p. 312, cf. vol. iii. p. 181.

this category.

I have now remarked on eight out of Mr. Goldenweizer's ten categories of differences between British Columbian and South Australian totemism; all of them, I think, are separable accidents of totemism; and most of them are easily to be accounted for by actual differences of culture, of social conditions, and by variety of savage taste and fancy in making guesses as to why totemists are totemistic.

IV.

We next arrive at the two first of Mr. Goldenweizer's categories. These are concerned with points of such very wide diffusion in the totemic world that I, under correction, take leave to regard them as "normal," while I hold that such variations from the norm as exist can be explained—as aberrations.

The first of these two categories is announced as:

BRITISH COLUMBIA.

1. Exogamy ⎰ Totemic phratries (Tlingit).
⎱ Totemic clans (Haida, Tsimshian, Northern Kwakiutl).

CENTRAL AUSTRALIA.

2. Exogamy ⎰ Phratries.
Classes.
Totem clans (generally not independent exogamous units).

This needs explanation! By "totemic *phratries*" in the case of the Tlingits, Mr. Goldenweizer means the two main exogamous divisions of the tribe, Wolf and Raven. By "totemic *clans*," in the case of the Haida, he also means the two main exogamous divisions, Raven and Eagle, which, really, are phratries. But it is also clear that Mr. Goldenweizer is here using the word "clans" as it exists in the peculiar terminology of Dr. Swanton. Mr. Goldenweizer informs us that "Dr. Swanton now fully recognises the strict parallelism of the social units of the Tlingit and Haida, and sanctions the use of 'phratry' and clan in both cases." This terminological source of confusion happily disappears.

We are now, alas, entering a region where the variations of evidence, the confusions of terminology, and the influence of wealth and rank in the creation of heraldry, cause extreme perplexity. Meanwhile, as the Haida "clans" of the category are, in fact, phratries; on the other hand the "totemic clans" of the Tsimshians and Northern Kwakiutl (Raven, Eagle, Hawk, Wolf), and six "totemic clans" of the Northern Kwakiutl seem destitute of phratries, which, among the Arunta of Central Australia, have also died out Mr. Goldenweizer, however, assigns phratries to Central Australia, the Arunta have none;[13] also "totem clans," where there are none, for the totemically named associations of the Arunta are not "clans," in the normal and usual sense of that word; they are not kins but associations.

---

[13] That is, the matrimonial classes, eight in all, are divided into two sets of four each, but these sets are nameless.

Mr. Goldenweizer, in his first category, speaks of Central Australia as possessing totemic "clans" ("generally not independent exogamous units"). If by "Central Australia" he means the Arunta group of tribes, they have, I repeat, no "totemic clans"; they have only clubs with totemic names, and these associations are not "exogamous units." Where phratries with totem kins in them exist, no totem kin is or can be "an independent exogamous unit," except where one totem to one totem marriage prevails, as among certain Australian tribes. But if the phratry rule be dropped, as Morgan says it was among the Iroquois, then people may marry into any totem kin except their own, and each totem kin becomes an "independent exogamous unit."[14]

Thus the first category in Mr. Goldenweizer's list needs a good deal of explanation and criticism.

The second category is *Totemic Names*. Under these, in British Columbia, are:

"Phratries (Tlingit)."
"Clans (Haida)." (But these are phratries.)
"Two of four clan Tsimshian."
"Clans (Northern Kwakiutl)."

In place of two animal-named clans out of four, Mr. Frazer assigns four animal-named clans to the Tsimshians;[15] Raven, Eagle, Wolf, and Bear. (*T. and E.*, vol. iii. pp. 307-308.) Mr. Goldenweizer himself[16] also assigns these *four animal-named clans to the Tsimshians*. But, in his table,[17] he docks two Tsimshian clans of their

---

[14] L. A. Morgan, *League of the Iroquois*, pp. 79-83.

[15] I may be permitted to note that these four Tsimshian clans look, to me, as if they had originally been two pairs of phratries. We find a parallel Australian case in the Narran-ga tribe of York's peninsula in South Victoria. Here Mr. Howitt gives us the "classes" (his term for phratries):

Kayi	Emu.
Waui	Red Kangaroo.
Wiltu	Eagle Hawk.
Wilthathu	Shark.

Each of these four main divisions had totem kins within it, and, as usual, the same totem (all are animals) never occurred in more than one main division. (Howitt, *N.T.S.E.A.* p. 130.) In precisely the same way "crests" of animal name occur in each of the four Tsimshian "clans":

Raven	Raven, Codfish, Starfish.
Eagle	Eagle, Halibut, Beaver, Whale.
Wolf	Wolf, Crane, Grizzly Bear.
Bear	Killer Whale, Sun, Moon, Stars, Rainbow, Grouse, and Sea Monster.

These "crests," thus arranged, no crest in more than one clan (or phratry?) look like old totems in the two pairs of clans, or, as I suspect, of phratries. The Australian parallel corroborates the view that the Tsimshian "clans" have been phratries.

[16] *J. A. F.* p. 187. quoting "Swanton 26th *B. E. R.*, 1904-1905, p. 423."

[17] *Ibid.* p. 229.

totem names. He does so also in his p. 190. Thus (p. 187) all of the four Tsimshian "clans" have animal names. But (p. 190), and also in the tabular arrangement, only two of the Tsimshian clans have animal names. Mr. Frazer gives to all four Tsimshian clans the names of animals. Whom are we to believe[18] Method is here a little to seek.

A much more serious puzzle meets us when, in his second category (totemic names), Mr. Goldenweizer assigns no totemic names to the "clans" of the Tlingit, while Mr. F. Boas (whose list is quoted by Mr. Frazer) and Holmberg (1856) do assign totemic names to the Tlingit clans.

Let us examine this situation.

If we take a South-East Australian tribe of the Barkinji pattern, we find it divided into two animal-named intermarrying phratries (or exogamous intermarrying "classes" or "moieties," I call them "phratries"). In each phratry are totem kins, that is, kins named after animals, vegetables, or other things in nature. The names of phratries and totem kins (I know no other word for them but totem kins or totem clans) descend in the female line. No such totem kin occurs in *both* exogamous phratries, therefore all these units are necessarily exogamous.

Two-thirds of the Australian phratry names are untranslated, like those of the Dieri; the other third, with a single exception (the Euahlayi), are names of animals.[19]

Now turn to the disputable case of the Tlingits of British Columbia. I first examine Mr. Frazer's account of them in Totemism and Exogamy (vol. iii. pp. 264-278). The Tlingits are divided into two exogamous phratries, or "classes," of animal names, Raven and Wolf. (In the north the Wolf "class" is also known as the Eagle.) Phratry exogamy is the rule; descent is in the female line. Each phratry is subdivided into a number of "clans," which are named after various animals. As no "clan" is represented in both phratries, and as all folk are obliged to marry out of their own phratry, the "clans" are, inevitably, exogamous.

For purposes of comparison with other British Columbia tribes, I give the list of Tlingit totem kins furnished by Mr. Frazer, "on the authority of Mr. F. Boas"[20]:

RAVEN PHRATRY.	WOLF (EAGLE) PHRATRY.
Raven.	Wolf.
Frog.	Hear.
Goose.	Eagle.
Sea Lion.	Killer Whale.
Owl.	Shark.
Salmon.	Auk.

---

[18] The truth seems to be that Mr. Goldenweizer (p. 189) misquotes Mr. Swanton, who (26th *B. E. R.* p. 423) is speaking, not of the Tsimshian but of the Haida. In his p. 190 Mr. Goldenweizer is quoting Dr. Boas, *Annual Archaeological Report,* Toronto, 1905, pp. 235-249.

[19] Thomas, *Kinship and Marriage in Australia.*

[20] *T. and E.,* vol. iii. p. 266, note 1.

Beaver.	Gull.
Codfish.	Sparrow Hawk.
Skate.	Thunder Bird.[21]

As I found out, and proved, in many Australian tribes the name of each phratry also occurs as the name of a totem kin in the phratry; so also it is among the Tlingit—*teste* Mr F. Boas.[22]

Thus on every point—female descent, animal-named phratries, animal-named totem kins, and each phratry containing a totem kin of its own name, the Tlingit totemism is absolutely identical with that of many South-Eastern Australian tribes of the most archaic type.

But the Tlingit, unlike the Australians, live in villages, and "the families or households may occupy one or more houses. The *families* actually take their names from places." (I italicise the word "families.") Mr. Frazer's authorities here are Holmberg (1856), Pauly (1862), Petroff ("the principal clans are those of the Raven, the Bear, the Wolf, and the Whale"), Krause (both here undated). Dr. Boas (1889). and Mr. Swanton (1908).

Mr Goldenweizer[23] does not mention that the "clans" of the Tlingit have animal names. Quite the reverse; he says that "the 'clans' of the Tlingit ... bear, with a few exceptions, names derived from localities."[24] This is repeated on p. 225.

At this point, really, the evidence becomes unspeakably perplexing. Mr. Frazer, we see, follows Mr. F. Boas and Holmberg (1856) in declaring that the "clans" of the Tlingit bear animal names. Mr. Goldenweizer says that, "with few exceptions," the "clans" of the Tlingit bear "names derived from localities."[25] Mr. Goldenweizer's authority is "Swanton, *Bur. Eth. Rep.*, 1904-1905 (1908), p. 398." Mr. Frazer[26] also quotes that page of Mr. Swanton, but does not say that Mr. Swanton here gives *local*, not animal, names to the clans of the Tlingit. Mr. Frazer also cites Mr. Swanton's p. 423 *sq.* Here we find Mr. Swanton averring that Killer Whale, Grizzly Bear, Wolf, and Halibut are in the Wolf phratry, "on the Wolf side," among the Tlingit; while Raven, Frog, Hawk, and Black Whale are on the Raven side. Here are animal names (not precisely as in Mr. Boas' list) within the phratries. But Mr. Swanton does not reckon these animal names as names of "clans"; to "clans" he gives local names in almost every case. To his mind these animal names in Tlingit society denote "*crests*" not "*clans*" and with crests we enter a region of confusion.

I cannot but think that the confusion is caused (apart from loose terminology) by the *crests* of these peoples. The crests are an excrescence, a heraldic result of wealth and rank; and as such can have nothing to do with early totemism. Scholars sometimes say "totems" when they mean "crests" (and perhaps *vice versa*), and confusion must ensue.

[21] T. and E., vol. iii. p. 266, note I.
[22] *Secret of the Totem*, pp. 164-170.
[23] *J. A. F.* p. 186.
[24] *J. A. F.* p. 190.
[25] *J. A. F.* pp. 190-225.
[26] *T. and E.*, vol. iii. p. 266, note 1.

I quote, on this point, a letter which Mr. Goldenweizer kindly wrote to me (Jan. 21, 1911).

"Since the appearance of Mr. Swanton's studies of the Tlingit and the Haida there remains no doubt whatever that the clans of these two tribes bear (with some few exceptions) names derived from localities. On pp. 398-9-400 of his Tlingit study (26th Report of the Bureau of American Ethnology, 1904-5) he gives a list of the geographical groups, and of the clans with their local names, classified according to the two phratries: Raven and Wolf. It must be remembered that to many of these clans he gives the totems [crests] of the Tlingit phratries: then the gentes [clans] of the Stikin tribe are enumerated. Some of the native names are translated as house or local names; it is pointed out that the raven occurs four times as the crest of four gentes [clans] with different names which, therefore, cannot mean 'raven.'

"The Haida case is quite parallel. Here 'each clan [phratry] was subdivided into a considerable number of families [clans] which generally took their names from some town or camping-place.' And again: 'It would seem that originally each family occupied a certain place or lived in a certain part of a town' (Swanton, *The Haida*, pp. 66, *sq.*) Now, of course, many clans are represented in several districts. Opposite p. 76 we find a genealogical table of the Raven families [clans] descended from Foam Woman, with their local names. A similar table of the Eagle families [clans] descended from Greatest Mountain, is given on p. 93. Again Professor Boas' account, although fragmentary, is correct. 'The phratries of the Haida are divided into gentes [clans] in the same way as those of the Tlingit, they also take their names, in the majority of cases, from the houses' (R.B.A.S., p. 822). The names of the Skidigate-village-people clans are given as an example.

"As to personal names among the Haida, a curious fact must be noted. Notwithstanding the greater prominence of crests and art among the Haida, their personal names are but seldom derived from animals, as is the rule among the Tlingit, the clans are not now restricted to one village district, but are found in several of the geographical groups. Thus the G ā n A x Á d î (of the Raven phratry) are found in the Tongas, Taku, Chilkat and Yakutat groups, while the Tégoedî (of the Wolf phratry) occur in the Tongas, Sanya, Hutsnuwù and Yakutat groups. The only non-local clan-names in the list are the Kuxînédî (marten people) of Henya; the SAgutēnedî (grass people) and NēsÁdî (salt-water people) of Kake; the LlūklnAxAdî (king-salmon people) of Sitka; and the LugāxAdî (quick people) of Chilkat. Each of these five clans occurs only once in the list, from which we may perhaps infer that they are of relatively late origin (this merely as a suggestion). On the other hand, 'the great majority of Tlingit personal names,' Mr. Swanton tells us, 'referred to some animal, especially that animal whose emblem was particularly valued by the clan to which the bearer belonged' (Bureau, 1904-5, pp. 421-2). In the passage you note, viz. 'the transposition of phratries is indicated also by crests and names, for the killer-whale, grizzly bear, wolf, and halibut, are on the Wolf side among the Tlingit and on the Raven side among the Haida, etc.,' the animals cited are the 'crests' while the 'names' referred to are, of course, the personal names which are derived from animals and as a rule change with the crests; therefore, they are not illustrated in the passage.

"Professor Boas' list is incomplete but similar in substance (Reports of the British Association for the Advancement of Science, 1889. p. 821). First majority of Haida personal names refer to the potlatch, property, etc. (Swanton, *The Haida*, pp. 119-120.) This is, no doubt, due to the influence of the potlatch which is among these people the central social and ceremonial feature.

"Holmberg's work I did not see. Probably his list of animals also stands for the crests and not the clan names....

"Of the Tsimshian clans only two bear animal names. K'anhada and Gyispo-tuwE'da do not, as Professor Boas formerly supposed, mean 'raven' and 'bear' (cf. R.B.A.A.S., 1889. p. 823 and Annual Archaeological Report, Toronto, 1906, p. 239)."

If I may ask a question about this very perplexing state of affairs, I would say, Is the animal crest of each "clan" supposed to be *later* than the local designation of the clan? To me it seems that the crest is in origin a heraldic representation of the clan totem, and that, as in Australia, totemic names of clans are older than names derived from localities or "houses." The house, the fixed building, is part of a society later than the first bearing of totemic names by clans. The crest, as a badge of rank and wealth, is later than the totem; social advance, houses, towns, heraldry, as a mark of rank, appear to me to cause the perplexities, and to place these American tribes outside of the totemism of people without rank, wealth, and houses and heraldry.

As I understand the case, the Tlingit clans did not originally, as Dr. Swanton seems to suppose, "occupy a certain place or live in a certain quarter of a town," whence they derived the place-names or town-names which they at present bear, according to Dr. Swanton. The Tlingit, now living in towns, and with clans of town-names, may naturally fancy that from the first their clans bore local or town-names. But society that begins in people who, like the Tlingit, have female descent, cannot form a local clan of descent, unless the men go to the homes of the women, which is not here the case. Originally I think their crests, as in Holmberg's report, were effigies of their clan totems, and the clans bore their totem names. But with advance to wealth, houses, and settled conditions, the local or town-names (as in other cases is certain) superseded the totem names of the clans, while the totem badge became, as the crest, a factor in a system of heraldry, to us perplexing. Certainly the facts as given by Dr. Swanton, may be envisaged in this way; the processes of change are simple, natural and have parallels elsewhere.

If a totemic clan chooses to wear the image of its totem as a badge, and has no other badge, all is plain sailing. But in British Columbia, as in Central British New Guinea, men, in proportion to their wealth and descent, wear an indefinite number of badges or "crests." "Although referred to by most writers as totems," says Mr. Swanton, speaking of the Haida tribe, "these crests have no proper totemic significance, their use being similar to that of the quarterings in heraldry, to mark the social position of the wearers."[27] Of course Australian totemists have no social position to be indicated by crests or badges. Now Dr. Boas speaks of "crests" as "totems," among the Haida,[28] and we are perplexed among these mixtures of

[27] Quoted, *T. and E.*, vol. iii. p. 281.

[28] *T. and E.*, vol. iii. p. 283.

heraldic with totemic terms.

Next, and this is curious, while Mr. Swanton gives local names to the "clans" of the Tlingit; to many but not all of his "House Groups" he gives *animal* names, "Raven, Moose, Grizzly Bear, Killer Whale, Eagle, Frog *houses*" and so on. All these animals are names of Holmberg's and Mr. F. Boas' totems of clans; but, according to Mr. Swanton, they are names borne, not by "clans" but by "house groups."[29] Other house groups have local names, or descriptive names, or nicknames, as "gambling house." Thus Mr. Frazer gives animal names to the "clans" of the Tlingit to which Mr. Swanton gives local names, and while many of the houses, or "house groups" of Mr. Swanton's Tlingit bear totemic names, Mr. Frazer says "the families generally take their names from places."[30] There appears to be confusion due to imperfect terminology.

Mr. Goldenweizer avers that "the intensive and prolonged researches conducted by a number of well trained observers among these tribes of the North Pacific border have shown with great clearness,"—something not at present to the point[31] But we regret the absence of clearness. Can we rely on Holmberg who described the state of affairs as it was fifty years ago, and who knew nothing, I presume, of Australian phratries and totem kins? In his time the Tlingit, like a dozen South-Eastern tribes of Australia, had animal-named kins in animal-named exogamous intermarrying phratries with female descent. Or was Holmberg (and was Mr. F. Boas in his list of animal-named Tlingit clans) led astray by the "crests"? Did each of these inquirers mistake "crests" for totems of clans?

One thing is clear, the Tlingit and the other tribes being possessed of wealth, and of gentry, and of heraldry, cause almost inextricable confusion by their use of heraldic badges, named "crests" by some; and "totems" (or *both* crests and totems at once) by other well trained observers. I am inclined to believe that most of these crests were, originally, representations of the totems of distinct totem kins. My reason is this: Mr. Swanton tells us that "the crests and names which among the Tlingit are on the Wolf side" are "on the Raven side" among the Haida. Among these people, animal names and crests are divided between the two phratries, the same name or crest not occurring in both phratries. This is merely the universal arrangement of totems in phratries.

Even now, among the Tlingit, says Mr. Swanton, "theoretically *the emblems*" (crests) "*used on the Raven side were different from those on the Wolf or Eagle side*," (precisely as, in Australia, the totems in Eagle Hawk phratry are different from those in Crow phratry), "and although a man of high caste might borrow an emblem from his brother-in-law temporarily, he was not permitted to retain it" (His brother-in-law, of course, was of the phratry not his own.) All this means no more than that occasionally a man of high caste may *now* impale the arms of his wife.[32] With castes and heraldry, born of wealth and rank, we have stepped out of totemism at this point It has been modified by social conditions. "Some families

---

[29] *Ber. Eth. Report*, 1904-1905, pp. 400-407.
[30] *T. and E.*, vol. iii. p. 266.
[31] *J. A. F.*, p. 287.
[32] *R. B. E., ut supra*, p. 415.

were too poor to have an emblem," did they also cease to have a totem? Some of the rich "could," it was said, "use anything." Is this because they pile up sixteen quarterings? "The same crest may be, and is, used by different clans, and any one clan may have several crests...."[33] Many "clans" now use the same crest, and there are quarrels about rights to this or that "crest." Some members of the Wolf phratry assert a right to the Eagle crest. Mr. Frazer thinks that "such claims are perhaps to be explained by marriages of the members of the clan with members of other clans who had these animals for their crests."[34]

That is precisely my own opinion. If "crests" were originally mere representations of each person's totem animal they have now become involved, through rank and social degrees, with heraldry, and with badges not totemic, such as a certain mountain. Meanwhile all the Tlingit "clans," if we follow Mr. Swanton's evidence, or almost all the "clans" are now mere local settlements, at least they bear local and other descriptive names. I nearly despair of arriving at Mr. Swanton's theory of what a Tlingit "clan" really is! But he gives a list of "the geographical groups," the "clans," and the phratry to which each of the clans belonged....

Thus we have (1)

Phratry Raven.

Then (2)

Tongas (I take Tongas to be "a geographical group").

Then under Tongas GānAXA'di, People of Gā'NAX.

Phratry Wolf.
    Tongas (Geographical group, apparently).
    Te'goedî, People of the island Teq°.

GānAXÁdî and Te'goedî seem to be "clans," but then clan Te'goedî, "People of the isle Teq°," looks like "a geographical group"!

There are fourteen "geographical divisions" of this kind, and sixty-eight "clans" of this kind, with descriptive or local names. The clans "were in a way local groups," says Mr. Swanton. They were also "clans or consanguineal bands," each "usually named from some town or camp it had once occupied." They "differed from the geographical groups ... being social divisions instead of comprising the accidental occupants of one locality."[35]

Be it observed that Mr. Swanton speaks of "these geographical divisions or tribes"; which increases the trouble, for, if the Tlingit be a "tribe," and the geographical divisions of the Tlingit be also "tribes," things are perplexing.

Once more, the Tlingit reckon descent in the female line. Now how can "a consanguineal band," which reckons descent in the female line, look like "a geographical group"? A totem kin, with male descent, in Australia and elsewhere, like a Highland clan, say the MacIans, necessarily becomes "a geographical group,"

---

[33] *T. and E.*, vol. iii. p. 268.
[34] *T. and E.*, vol. iii. p. 269.
[35] *R. B. E. ut supra*, p. 398.

say in Glencoe. But how, with female descent (unless the women go to the men's homes), a Tlingit "consanguineal band" can also have a local habitation is to me a difficult question. The names of the phratries descend in the female line. Do the local and descriptive names of "the clans or consanguineal bands," also descend in the female line? I cannot presume to say. Mr. Frazer throws no light on this point believing, as he does, that the "clans" within the Tlingit phratries, are the familiar totem kins, of animal names. If so, the children must inherit the maternal totem "clan" name.

Only one thing is clear to me, a Tlingit of the Wolf phratry can only marry a bride of the Raven phratry; a Tlingit of the Raven phratry can only woo a maiden of the Wolf phratry. If totem kins there be in the phratries, these totem kins are exogamous. If there be no totem kins in the phratry, are Mr. Swanton's clans of local names *locally* exogamous? May persons marry within the region where they are settled? I know not, but I rather incline to suppose that members of *both* phratries may be found in Mr. Swanton's clans of local name; indeed it *must* be so, and therefore a pair of lovers *may* perhaps wed *within* their "clan or consanguineal band," and within their local group, which, thus, is not exogamous. If so, the Tlingit clan is *not* exogamous. But all *this* is purely conjectural.

While, in Mr. Swanton's version, the Tsimshians, with female descent, have two exogamous "clans" with animal names, and two with other names; while in Mr. Frazer's book they have four animal-named exogamous clans, there is a third story resting on the authority of Mr. William Duncan, a missionary among the Tsimshian from 1857 onwards.[36] Mr. Duncan's information Commander Mayne incorporated in his book.[37]

According to Commander Mayne, using Mr. Duncan's evidence, in 1862, the Tsimshians (as we have seen), carved faces of "Whale, Porpoise, Raven, Eagle, Wolf, Frog, etc.," on roof beams. He calls such effigies "crests." No person may marry another of the same "crest": the children take their mother's *crest*, and bear the name of the animal which it represents. None may kill the animal of his crest. All this is exogamy with totem kins, under the phratries, as the exogamous units,[38] and with the totemic taboo. If Mayne and Duncan are right, either more recent writers are wrong, or Tsimshian totemism has been much modified since 1862.

[36] Mayne, *Four Years in British Columbia*, p. 257 *sq.* 1862.
[37] See *T. and E.*, vol. iii. pp. 309-311.
[38] *T. and E.*, vol. iii. pp. 309-311.

V.

Further south than the Tsimshian dwell the Kwakiutl, of whom the most southerly are called "the Kwakiutl proper." The northern Kwakiutl are divided, says Dr. Boas, into "septs" and "clans." What a "sept" may be I am not certain. The first tribe has "clans" called Beaver, Eagle, Wolf, Salmon, Raven, Killer Whale: the usual totemic names in this region. These totemic clans are exogamous, like those of Mayne's Tsimshians. Descent is in the female line. In the next tribe we find three exogamous animal-named clans: Eagle, Raven, Killer Whale, Beaver, Wolf, and Salmon have vanished, or have never existed. In these two tribes a child is sometimes placed in the father's, not in the mother's clan, as a Dieri father sometimes "gives" his totem to his son, in addition to the inherited maternal totem.[39]

When we reach the southern Kwakiutl ("the Kwakiutl proper") we are told by Dr. Boas that "patriarchate prevails." This appears to mean that descent is here reckoned not, as in the north, in the female, but in the male line. "We do not find a single clan that has, properly speaking, an animal for its totem; neither do the clans take their name from their crest, nor are there phratries."[40] As the *northern* Kwakiutl have animal-named exogamous "clans" with female descent, Dr. Boas now thinks that the *northern* Kwakiutl "have to a great extent adopted the maternal descent and the division into animal totems of the northern tribes."[41] We do not know, elsewhere, that totemism has ever been borrowed by one tribe from another, especially by a tribe so advanced in culture as the Kwakiutl, and we have no example of a tribe in which the men have given up their social prerogatives, and transmitted them to their nephews in the female line.

Mr. Frazer writes, "The question naturally arises, Are the Kwakiutl passing from maternal institutions to paternal institutions, from mother-kin to father-kin, or in the reverse direction?... In one passage Dr. Boas seems to incline to the former member of this alternative, that is, to the view that the Kwakiutl are passing, or have passed, from mother-kin, or (as he calls it) matriarchate to father-kin or patriarchate, for he says that "the marriage ceremonies of the Kwakiutl seem to show that originally matriarchate prevailed also among them."[42] Yet he afterwards adopted with great decision the "contrary view." On these very intricate problems I take leave to quote the statement with which Mr. Goldenweizer has been good enough to favour me.

---

[39] *T. and E.*, vol. iii. pp. 318, 319.

[40] *Fifth Report on N. W. Tribes of Canada*, 1890. *T. and E.*, vol. iii. p. 320, note 1.

[41] *Twelfth Report on N. W. Tribes of Canada*, 1898, p. 676. *T. and E.*, vol. iii. p. 320, note 1.

[42] *T. and E.*, vol. iii. p. 332, citing Dr. Boas in *Fifth Report on N. W. Tribes of Canada*, p. 33, 1889.

First, as to descent among the Kwakiutl proper.

"At first, as Mr. Frazer points out (iii. p. 329 *sq.*). Dr. Boas believed that the Kwakiutl were passing from maternal to paternal descent. Later investigations conducted by Dr. Farrand (cf. F. Boas, *The Mythology of the Bella Coola*, Jesup North Pacific Expedition, vol. i. p. 121), led to a reversal of that opinion. The main arguments for original paternal descent among the Kwakiutl are three in number. (1) The village communities, which were the original social unit of the Kwakiutl,[43] regarded themselves as direct descendants of a mythical ancestor, and not as descendants of the ancestor's sister, which is the case in the legends of the northern tribes, with maternal descent. (Cf. F. Boas, *The Kwakiutl*, etc., p. 335, where a genealogy is also given.) (2) A number of offices connected with the ceremonies of the secret societies, such as master of ceremonies, etc., are hereditary in the male line (F. Boas, *Kwakiutl*, etc., p. 431). The Secret Societies, with their dances, are a very ancient institution among the Kwakiutl, and the male inheritance of the above offices is a strong argument for the former prevalence of paternal descent among these people. (3) The form taken by the maternal inheritance of rank, privileges, etc., among the Kwakiutl points in the same direction. When a man marries he receives crests, privileges, etc., from his father-in-law through his wife, but he himself may not use them but must keep them for his son, who, when of proper age, may sing the songs, perform the dances, use the crest, etc., which he thus receives from his mother through the medium of his father. (Cf. F. Boas, *Kwakiutl*, etc., p. 334.) When the young man marries he must return his privileges to his father, who then gives them to his daughter when she marries. Thus, son-in-law No. 2 receives the privileges, but again may not use them, but keeps them for his son, etc. It appears, then, that the privileges exercised by the young man before marriage are always derived from his mother, but formally he receives them from his father, who acts as a sort of guardian of these privileges until the son is ready for them. Descent here is clearly maternal, but the form of paternal descent is preserved, a plausible condition for a people who; having become maternal, still stick at least in form to the traditional inheritance from the father. If this inference be rejected, the feature becomes quite unaccountable.

"In the sentence, 'The woman's father, on his part, has acquired his privileges in the same manner through his mother' (Frazer, vol. iii. p. 333. note i), the privileges the woman's father exercised as a young man before marriage are meant. The privileges he later acquired through his wife he, of course, could not use, but had to keep them for his son. The phrase, 'each individual inherits the crest of his maternal grandfather' (Frazer, iii. p. 331, note 2), must be similarly interpreted. The crest the individual uses before marriage is meant.

"In connection with the foregoing it must be remembered that another mode of acquiring privileges, crests, songs, etc., was common among the Kwakiutl, viz. by killing the owner (cf. F. Boas, *Kwakiutl*, etc., p. 424, and elsewhere).

"I also cite the actual words of Dr. Boas. He believes that the intricate law by which 'a purely female line of descent is secured, although only through the medi-

[43] It seems to me impossible to suppose that the village community was ever anywhere "the original social unit." —A. L.

um of the husband,' can only be explained 'as an adaptation of maternal laws by a tribe which was on a paternal stage. I cannot imagine that it is a transition of a maternal society to a paternal society, because there are no relics of the former' (maternal) 'stage beyond those which we find everywhere, and which do not prove that the transition has been recent at all. There is no trace left of an inheritance from the wife's brothers; the young people do not live with the wife's parents. But the most important argument is that the customs cannot have been prevalent in the village communities from which the present tribal system originated, as in these' (village communities) 'the tribe is always designated as the direct descendants of the mythical ancestor. If the village communities had been on the maternal stage, the tribes would have been designated as the descendants of the ancestor's sisters, as is always the case in the legends of the northern tribes.'"[44]

From all this it appears that Dr. Boas believes the Kwakiutl proper to have been once, "on the maternal stage," of which the usual "relics" survive, but why should *all* such traces survive? Some must disappear, otherwise there could be no transition!

Apparently, in the village communities, the existence of a mythical *ancestor*, not *ancestress*, is postulated; while in the northern tribes, with female descent, mythical *ancestresses* are postulated. But if, among the Kwakiutl proper, male ancestry is now the recognised rule (and it dimly seems to be so), then, as usual, Kwakiutl myth will throw back into the unknown past the institutions of their present state, will say "ancestor," not "ancestress." No argument can be based on traditions which are really explanatory conjectures. There is advanced no valid reason for supposing that the Kwakiutl proper began with descent in the female line, then advanced to the male line, and then doubled back on the female line, and so evolved transmission of crests in the female line, through husbands.

The waverings of the Kwakiutl between the two lines of descent are, in fact, such as we expect to occur when a people has retained, like the Tlingit, Haida, and Tsimshians, the system of female descent after reaching a fair pitch of physical culture, and arriving at wealth, rank, and the attribution of children to the paternal stock.

---

[44] *Rep. U.S. Nat. Museum*, 1897. pp. 334-335.

VI.

I now come to give my own opinion as to the ways in which Kwakiutl totemism may have attained its existing peculiarities. It is necessary first to defend my view that the essential thing in totemism — surveying the whole totemic field — is the existence of exogamous kins bearing animal and other such names. Here Mr. Goldenweizer opposes me, saying that "no particular set of features can be taken as characteristic of totemism, for the composition of the totemic complex is variable, nor can any particular feature be regarded as fundamental, for not one of the features does invariably occur in conjunction with others; nor is there any evidence to regard any other feature as primary in order of development, or as of necessity original psychologically."[45]

I have already remarked that this is true; we find human *associations*, which are *not* kins or clans, bearing animal and other totemic names, while these associations are not exogamous (the Arunta nation); and we find exogamous sets, kins, or associations which do not bear animal names.

But the co-existence of the exogamous kin with the totemic name of that kin is found in such an immense and overwhelming majority over every other arrangement; the exogamous "totem clan" is so hugely out of proportion in numbers and width of diffusion over the Arunta animal-named non-exogamous associations and other rare exceptions, that we have a right to ask — Are not the exceptions aberrant variations? Have not the Arunta, with non-exogamous sets bearing totemic names, and other peoples with exogamous sets *not* of totemic names, passed through and out of the usual stage of animal-named exogamous kins? A mere guess that this is so, that the now non-exogamous human sets with totem names have once been exogamous, would be of no value. I must prove, and fortunately I can prove, that it *was* so.

It is certain, historically, that some exogamous units which now bear non-totemic names, in the past were ordinary totem kins with totemic names. As we can also demonstrate to a certainty that the Arunta have been in, and, for definite reasons, have passed out of, the ordinary stage of exogamous totem kins, we have a right, I think, to say that, normally, the feature of the totemic name is associated with the feature of exogamy, and that the exceptions really prove the rule, for we can show how the exceptions came to vary from the rule.

Mr. Goldenweizer, in a very brief criticism of my own theory of Totemism, given by me in *Social Origins* (1903), and in *The Secret of the Totem* (1905), writes "Why is the question, How did the early groups come to be named after the plants and animals? — the real problem? Would not Lang admit that other features may

[45] *J. A. F.* pp. 269, 270.

also have been the starting point?" (I not only admit but insist that "other features" were among the starting-points of exogamous totemism.) Among "the other features" Mr. Goldenweizer gives "animal taboos, or a belief in descent from an animal, or primitive hunting regulations, or what not? I am sure that Lang, who is such an adept in following the *logos,* could without much effort construct a theory of totemism with any one of these elements to start with—a theory as consistent with fact, logic, and the mind of primitive man, as is the theory of names accepted from without."

Now as to the last point, I have written "unessential to my system is the question *how* the groups got animal names, as long as they got them and did not remember how they got them" (*et seq.*)[46] I *did* show how European and other village groups obtained animal names, namely as *sobriquets* given from without; and I proved the same origin of the modern names of Siouan "gentes," of two Highland clans; of political parties, religious sects; and so forth.

This mode of obtaining names is a *vera causa*: that is all: and nobody had remarked on it, in connection with totemism.

Next I cannot "without much effort" (or with any effort) construct a theory of totemism out of (1) "animal taboos." They are imposed for many known and some unknown reasons, and not all totem kins taboo the totem object. Next (2) as I must repeat that "belief in descent from an animal," is only one out of many post-totemic myths explanatory of totemism; I cannot possibly use it as the starting-point of totemism. If Mr. Goldenweizer has read the book which he is criticising, he forgets that I wrote[47] "it is an error to look for origins in myths about origins," and that I refused to accept as corroboration of my theory an African myth which agrees with my own view.

As to (3) "primitive hunting regulations," Mr. Goldenweizer does not tell us what they were. It is a very common "regulation" that no totem kin may hunt its own totem animal, but to suggest that the totem kin was created by the regulation is to mistake effect for cause.

Finally (4), who can take "or what not" for the starting-point of an investigation? But every totem kin has a totemic name: if there is no totemic name how can we know that we have before us a totem kin? If the Tlingit "clans" be exogamous but not named by totemic names (as Mr. Swanton tells us), then the Tlingit clans are not totemic, now, whatever they may have been in the past: and we are not concerned with them.

Of every totem "clan" the totem name is a *universal* feature; and therefore I must begin my study from what is universal—the names. Here (though we must not appeal to authority), I have the private satisfaction of being in agreement with Mr. Howitt. The assumption by men of the names of objects "in fact must have been the commencement of totemism," says Mr. Howitt.[48]

I start then, from the totemic names because,—no totemic name, no totem-

---

[46] *Secret of the Totem,* p. 125.

[47] *Secret of the Totem,* p. 23.

[48] *Native Tribes of South-East Australia,* p. 153.

ic "clan"! With the totemic name of a social unit in the tribe, I couple exogamy, (though exogamy may exist apart from totemism), because exogamy is always associated with a "clan" of totemic name, except in a very few cases of which the Arunta "nation" is much the most prominent. But it is not to the point, for *the Arunta have no totemic clans*. Mr. Frazer's latest definition of totemism is "an intimate relation which is supposed to exist between a group of *kindred* people on the one side and a species of natural or artificial objects on the other...."[49] Now the Arunta associations of animal names are not (I must keep repeating) kindreds, are not "clans," are not composed of persons who are, "humanly speaking," akin. The totem is not inherited from either parent or through any kinsman or kinswoman. The Arunta bearers of the same totem name, in each case, do not constitute a "clan." This puts the so-called Arunta "totem clans," non-exogamous, out of action as proofs that "totem clans" may be non-exogamous.

Moreover, the non-exogamous Arunta associations bearing totemic names have once been exogamous totem clans. The usages of the Arunta, and their traditions, and the actual facts of their society, prove that their totems were originally hereditary and exogamous.[50]

I use the word "prove" deliberately; the demonstration is of historical and mathematical certainty. These facts compel me to believe that the Arunta have been in and passed out of normal hereditary totemism, in which the totems are arranged so that no totem occurs in both main exogamous divisions, and all totems are exogamous. In that normal totemic stage the Arunta have at one time been. But they have passed out of it into their present "conceptional" totemism, with the same totems appearing in both main exogamous divisions, the totems being non-hereditary, and non-exogamous.

Spencer and Gillen say, "in the Arunta, as a general rule, the great majority of the members of any one totemic group belong to one moiety of the tribe, but this is by no means universal, and in different totemic groups certain of the ancestors are supposed to have belonged to one moiety and others to the other, with the result that of course their living descendants also follow their example."[51] (This statement I later compare with others by the same authors.) Now in normal totemism, not "the great majority," but all the members of any one totemic group belong to one or other moiety of the tribe. The totems being hereditary, they cannot wander out of their own into the other phratry, and, as all persons must marry out of their own phratry, they cannot marry into their own totem, for no person of their own totem is in the phratry into which they must marry.

At present "the great majority" of members of each totem, among the Arunta, are in one phratry or the other. Thus their society is either, (1) in some unknown way, rapidly approximating itself to normal totemism, or (2) has comparatively recently emerged from normal totemism. The former alternative is impossible. Each Arunta obtains his or her totem by sheer chance, by the accident of the supposed locality of his or her conception, and of the totemic *erathipa* or *ratapa* which alone

---

[49] *T. and E.*, vol. iv. pp. 3, 4.
[50] What, follows I have already said in *Anthropos*, 1910.
[51] *Northern Tribes*, p. 175.

haunt that spot.[52] Manifestly this present Arunta mode of determining totems cannot introduce the great majority of each totem into one or the other phratry or main exogamous division (Panunga-Bulthara and Purula-Kumara), for these divisions have now no local habitation or limits. Consequently the arrangement by which the great majority of each totem is in one or the other moiety can be due to nothing but the fact that the Arunta have comparatively recently emerged from normal exogamous and hereditary, into conceptional, casual, non-hereditary and non-exogamous totemism. Had they emerged long ago, and adopted their present fortuitous method of acquiring the totem, *manifestly the totems, by the operation of chance, would now be present in almost equal numbers in both phratries*. This would also be the case had Arunta totemism always been conceptional and fortuitous.

According to Spencer and Gillen, "it is the idea of spirit individuals associated with *churinga* and resident in certain definite spots, that lies at the root of the present totemic system of the Arunta tribe."[53]

This is certainly true; and the facts prove, we shall see, to demonstration, that this actual "conceptional" state of Arunta totemism is later than, and has caused the disappearance of the normal hereditary exogamous totemism, among the Arunta.

It is plain and manifest that if the Arunta nation, from the first, were in their present stage of "conceptional totemism"—the totem of each individual being always determined by sheer chance—when the exogamous division of the tribe was instituted, individuals of each totem would be almost equally distributed between the two main divisions, Purula-Kumara and Bulthara-Panunga. Chance could not put the great majority of the members of every totem name either into one exogamous division or the other. If any one doubts this, let him take four packs of cards (208 cards), and deal them alternately five or six times to two friends, Jones representing the phratry Bulthara-Panunga, and Brown standing for the phratry Purula-Kumara. It will not be found that Brown always holds the great majority of Court cards—Ace, King, Queen and Knave—and the great majority of tens, nines and eights: while Jones holds the great majority of sevens, sixes, and fives, fours, threes, and twos.

Chance distribution does not keep on working in that way; and the chance conceptional distribution of totems could not put the great majority of, say, Kangaroos, Hachea Flowers, Wild Cats, and Little Hawks in the Bulthara-Panunga phratry, and the great majority of Emus, Lizards, Wichetty Grubs, and Dogs in the Purula-Kumara division. That is quite impossible. Yet all (or almost all) Arunta totems are thus distributed between the two main exogamous divisions.

When once the reader understands this fact—insisted on by Spencer and Gillen—he becomes convinced, becomes mathematically certain that the chance distribution of conceptional totemism did not and could not thus array the totems of the Arunta. This present arrangement, and this alone, makes the Arunta associations with totemic names non-exogamous. I proceed to give further evidence of Spencer and Gillen. "Whilst every now and then we come across traditions,

[52] Vol. i. pp. 189-190. *Central Tribes*, p. 123.
[53] *Central Tribes*, p. 123.

according to which, as in the case of the Achilpa," (Cats) "the totem is common to all classes[54] we always find that in each totem one moiety of the tribe predominates,[55] and that, according to tradition, many of the groups" (totem groups) "of ancestral individuals consisted originally of men or women or of both men and women, who all belonged to one moiety. Thus in the case of certain Okira or Kangaroo groups we find only Kumara and Purula; in certain Udnirringita or Wichetty Grub groups we find only Hulthara and Panunga, in certain Achilpa or 'Wild Cat' (groups) 'a predominance of Kumara and Purula, with a smaller number of Bulthara and Panunga.'[56] At the present day no totem is confined to either moiety of the tribe, but in each local centre we always find a great predominance of one moiety, as for example at Alice Springs, the most important centre of the Wichetty Grubs, amongst forty individuals, thirty-five belong to the Bulthara and Panunga and only five to the other moiety of the tribe."[57]

Here the great majority—thirty-five to five—of the members of the totem belong to one of the two main exogamous divisions. Outside of the Arunta nation and Kaitish all the Grubs would belong to one main exogamous division. It is mathematically certain that chance could not bring thirty-five to five members of a given totem—or, "a great majority" in each case—into one or other phratry.

Consequently the chance distribution of totems on the present conceptional Arunta system has not caused this uniform phenomenon. It follows that the totems of the Arunta were at one time hereditary, and were arranged, some exclusively in one, some exclusively in the other moiety, so that no person could marry into his or her own totem. The fortuitous system of conceptional distribution then arose out of the Arunta philosophy of spirits and emanations, and out of the *churinga nanja* usage, and has now detached a small minority of members of each totem from their original phratry and lodged them in the other. Members of every totem can therefore find legal spouses of their own totem in the phratry not their own, and may marry them. And thus these Arunta associations with totemic names are now non-exogamous. But they have been exogamous totem kins. Mr. Frazer finds what he calls totemism without exogamy in parts of Melanesia.[58] I need not here repeat my arguments, given in *Anthropos*, vol. v. (1910) pp. 1092-1108, to prove that the so-called "totems" in this case are only animal or vegetable "familiars" of individuals. Thus the great example of "totem clans" so-called, without exogamy, is put out of action. The Arunta "clans" are not clans, and the Arunta have had exogamous totem clans like other people.

[54] The myth is self-contradictory in the case of the Achilpa. They were in both phratries; the other totems were confined to one or the other phratry. In the latter case the myth exaggerates the present state of things, and puts all, not the great majority, of each totem in one phratry or the other. In the former case the myth throws the actual state of things back into the past.

[55] By "moiety" the authors mean one of the two main exogamous divisions or phratries.

[56] *Central Tribes*, p. 120. In fact out of three Achilpa or Wild Cat sets of wanderers, two, in the legend, are exclusively of one phratry—Purula-Kumara—and one is exclusively of the other, Bulthara-Panunga, *op. cit.* p. 120.

[57] *Central Tribes*, p. 120.

[58] *T. and E.*, vol. iii. pp. 9, 287.

VII.

We now turn to cases in which exogamous "clans" bear, not totemic names, but local or descriptive names, like the Tlingit according to Dr. Swanton. In several instances it is easy to prove that exogamous "clans," now bearing local or other descriptive names, have previously borne totemic names. This result has often been attained by the circumstance that *with male descent of the totem name*, a regular *local* clan is formed. Such a clan then comes to be known by a territorial description (just as lairds were in Scotland) and the totemic name may drop out of use. If so, the clan becomes exogamous under a territorial or other name, and is no longer a totem clan.

But this explanation cannot apply to the Tlingit, with female descent, for with female descent, unless the men go to the women's homes, no local clan of descent is possible. I have shown that I do not pretend to know precisely what are the facts of the Tlingit system, as accounts contradict each other. But in other American cases, as in those of the Apaches and Navahos, the tribes "are divided into a large number of exogamous clans with descent in the female line, but the names of the clans appear to be local, not totemic...."[59] Such names are Lone Tree, Red Flat, House of the Cliffs, Bend in a Canyon, and so forth. Are such names inherited? Is every child of a woman of Red Flat called "Red Flat"? Persons of the same clan or phratry (from eight to twelve phratries) may not intermarry. The phratries "have no formal names"; speaking of his phratry a man will often refer to it by the title of its oldest or most numerous clan—and that, it seems, is always a local name, "Dr. Washington Matthews," says Mr. Frazer, "who spoke with authority on the subject, was of opinion that the Navahos clans were originally and indeed till quite recently local exogamous groups and not true clans." What else can they be? But Dr. Washington Matthews found a legend which suggests that the Navahos were once totemic. If this be an explanatory myth its point is to explain *why the clans have now local names*, and why do the clans think that the fact needs explanation? " It is said that when they set out on their journey each clan was provided with a different pet, such as a bear, a puma, a deer, a snake, and a porcupine, and that when the clans received their local names these pets were set free."[60] That is, place-names ousted totem names.

It appears to me that when a tribe acquires settled habits and lives in villages, territorial names may oust totem names, and exogamy may become, as among the Navaho, local, just as it becomes local in several Australian tribes with male

---

[59] *T. and E.*, vol. iii, p. 243.

[60] *T. and E.* vol. iii. p. 245. note 5, citing Washington Matthews. *J. A. F.* iii., 1890, p. 105, and *Navaho Legends*, p. 31, 1897.

descent. But nothing in my theory compels me to suppose that every people has passed through totemic exogamy. Exogamy, in my view, was prior to totemism; totem names were a later way of designating local groups which were already exogamous.[61] "The rule would be, No marriage within the local group." The totemic names were a later addition, and I can think of no reason why all peoples should necessarily accept totemic names; only, as it chances, the enormous majority among the lower races have done so.

Perhaps the Navaho and Apaches never had totemic names for their exogamous local groups. They are not known to exhibit any sign or vestige of totemism beyond the legend or myth of the wild animal pets.

All such cases of exogamous units bearing non-totemic names, in tribes of female descent, where no vestige of totemism is found, are outside of the field of totemism. Why should we treat people as totemic who have no totems? If we held the opinion that totemism was the cause of exogamy, the position would be different. At one time I thought that the totem and the totem blood taboo, clinched, as it were, and sanctified a pre-existing exogamy. But as I never found that marriage within the totem was automatically punished by sickness or death; (as, in many tribes, the offence of eating the totem is supposed to be); I saw that marriage within the totem was a breach of secular law, punished capitally by "the State." There is no taboo in the case. But as we repudiate the opinion that totemism was the cause of exogamy, in studying totemism we have no concern with peoples who are exogamous but show no trace of having ever been totemic.

---

[61] *Secret of the Totem,* pp. 114, 115.

VIII.

The case of the Tlingit is quite different. Here the phratries have totemic names; the "clans" in the phratries are said, by early authorities, to have totemic names; the "crests" (mainly the same animals as those said to give names to the Tlingit "clans") are readily to be explained by totemism evolving into heraldry.

But, if the Tlingit clans have not totemic names, then it would appear that, among a people of dwellers in towns, local names of local groups have succeeded to totemic names of totemic kins. This can only occur where people have settled habitations, towns or villages, or where totem kins have been localised by male descent.

We know that, even among some of the Australian tribes with male descent, totem kins become local groups, and thus the predominant totem of each such group becomes attached to a locality, as among the Narran-ga of Yorke Peninsula. They had two pairs of phratries of animal names:

Emu.   Eagle Hawk.

Red Kangaroo.   Shark.

In each such phratry was a number of totem kins, the same totem never appearing in more than one phratry (or "class" in Mr. Howitt's term). Each class or phratry was limited to a certain territory: Emu to the north, Red Kangaroo to the east, Eagle Hawk to the west, and Shark to the extreme point of the peninsula (south). The totems, passing from father to son, were thus localised. They ceased to be exogamous—obviously because each man, to find a wife eligible on exogamous principles, had to travel to a place inconveniently remote. Thus the only restriction on marriage was "forbidden degrees" of consanguinity.[62]

All this is easily intelligible. Male descent fixed phratries and totems to localities. By the old rule, if Emu phratry had to marry into Shark phratry, the localities were at the extreme ends of the peninsula, north and south; the other two phratries were as far asunder as the cast of the peninsula is from the west. Consequently, though the old machinery of exogamy existed, the practice of exogamy was dropped: persons might marry within their own totem kins. But we are not told whether all four "classes" inter-married, or each "class" only with one other, because the old rule had fallen into disuse before the coming of Europeans.

Mr. Howitt gives a case of "the transfer of the prohibition of marriage within the totem, to the totem clan—that is, to the locality." In this case, that of the Narrinyeri, with male descent, most "clans" have a local name, or a nickname,

---

[62] Howitt, *N.T.S.E.A.*, pp. 124, 130, 258, 259.

and have totems. But three such units or "clans" out of twenty retain their totem names—Whale, Coot, Mullet—thus indicating that totemic preceded local names. A local "clan" may have as many as three totems, but in thirteen cases out of twenty each local clan had but one totem. Among nicknames are "Gone over there," and "Where shall we go?" These clans (thirteen out of twenty) having local names, were strictly exogamous. So also, of course, were the totems of the local clans; though, save in three cases, the name of the place of residence, or a nickname, had superseded the totem name as the title of the clan. It is as if, in place of speaking of the MacIans, we said "the Glencoe men"; instead of speaking of the Stewarts, said "the Appin men"; in place of speaking of the Camerons, said "the men of Lochaber."

Thus it by no means follows that if the exogamous "clans" of any tribe of the North-West Pacific have local names, therefore they never had totemic names, as many of them have to this day. The rise of settled towns or village communities yields a new set of conditions, and a new set of non-totemic names for the clans, in some cases; precisely as the localisation of a totem clan through the operation of male descent causes a local name to take the place, usually but not universally, of a totem clan name in Southern Victoria.

Consequently Mr. Goldenweizer can make no argumentative use of the alleged local names of the Tlingit clans. If the totemic names of exogamous units—showing connections with totemism in crests and totemic phratry names—be absent, that is because, under known conditions, they have been superseded by local names or nicknames. This process is a vera causa in totemic society.

IX.

I now give an American case, in which a tribe, the Mandans, exhibit female descent, exogamous clans, and a mixture of totemic clan names with local names or *sobriquets*. The people were settled, lived in villages or towns, "with houses very commodious, neat, and comfortable." The tribe was agricultural, growing maize, beans, pumpkins, and tobacco. Out of seven clan names four were totemic—Wolf, Bear, Prairie Chicken, Eagle; two—Flathead and Good Knife—look like nicknames; High Village is local.[63] Here we find other sorts of clan names encroaching on totem names.

Among the Crows, with exogamous clans and female descent, out of twelve clan names four are totemic—Prairie Dog, Skunk, Raven, Antelope; three are very unkind nicknames.[64]

The American tribes have been much disturbed by the whites, and many changes have occurred in their institutions. As Mr. Frazer points out, in a book of 1781 Captain Carver describes Siouan "bands" or "tribes" (really totem kins), each with a badge representing an animal, and named after the animals: Eagles, Panthers, Tigers, Buffaloes, Snakes, Tortoises, Squirrels, Wolves, etc. These people were Sioux or Dacotas; whether they were exogamous or not Carver does not say. But, in place of now bearing totemic names, the "gentes" of these people are at present distinguished by obvious and even odious nicknames, such as "Breakers of the Law," because members of this *gens* disregarded the marriage law by taking wives within the *gens*.

So says Mr. Dorsey. Mr. Frazer says the bands of this tribe are not exogamous. But they must have been exogamous when a gens received a nickname for breaking the law of exogamy. One "band" or *gens* "Eats no Geese"; it may have been a Goose clan. Other bands or *gentes* bear nicknames or local names.[65]

I need not give more examples. In America, as in Australia, various conditions, already mentioned, cause changes from totemic names of exogamous clans to local names and nicknames.

It has now been proved that though, in very rare cases, such as those of the Arunta and Narran-ga, sets of people may have totemic names, yet marry within the name; and that, though "clans" may be exogamous and yet bear names which are not totemic, nevertheless the co-existence of totemic names with exogamy prevails in the overwhelming majority of instances, while the exceptions, as they have

[63] *T. and E.*, vol. ill. pp. 135, 136. Morgan, *Ancient Society*, p. 158.
[64] *T. and E.*, vol. iii. pp. 153, 154.
[65] *T. and E.*, vol. iii. pp. 86, 87. Dorsey, *R.B.F.*, xv. (1897) *et seq.*

been accounted for by their causes, prove the rule. Consequently I see no error of method in holding that the totemic name and exogamy are normal features of totemism, while totemism is "an integral phenomenon."

This is my answer to Mr. Goldenweizer's criticisms. Of course I do not say that totemism was the cause of exogamy; I hold that exogamy was prior to totemism, and think it perfectly possible that some exogamous peoples may never have been totemic.

In this discussion I have, not illogically I hope, taken into account relative conditions of advancement among the peoples studied. I have not here shown that reckoning descent in the male line is a social advance on reckoning in the female line, but I am able to prove that it is, at least in Australia. I have shown that wealth, rank, and settled habitations tend to modify totemism, for example, by introducing heraldry, and enabling non-totemic to supersede, now more now less, the totemic names of exogamous units.

Mr. Goldenweizer, as we saw, writes "that these conditions are due to the fact that the tribes of British Columbia are 'advanced' cannot be admitted."[66] I am sorry that he cannot admit what is true and obvious. The wealth, the art, the degrees of rank, the settled houses and towns of the British Columbian tribes have introduced the perplexities of their heraldry; as in other parts of America and in Australia other causes have brought in local names for exogamous kins.

---

[66] *J. A. F.* p. 287.

Lector House believes that a society develops through a two-fold approach of continuous learning and adaptation, which is derived from the study of classic literary works spread across the historic timeline of literature records. Therefore, we aim at reviving, repairing and redeveloping all those inaccessible or damaged but historically as well as culturally important literature across subjects so that the future generations may have an opportunity to study and learn from past works to embark upon a journey of creating a better future.

This book is a result of an effort made by Lector House towards making a contribution to the preservation and repair of original ancient works which might hold historical significance to the approach of continuous learning across subjects.

HAPPY READING & LEARNING!

LECTOR HOUSE LLP
E-MAIL: lectorpublishing@gmail.com